NEW YORK CONTEMPORARY

GRADE ARCHITECTURE AND INTERIORS

THOMAS HICKEY & EDWARD YEDID

THE MONACELLI PRESS

Simon Baker GEORGE CONDO
JOSEPH DIRAND Interior

CONTENTS

IMPERIAL
Glory
EAMES
MANOLO VALDÉS
CHAMBORD

INTRODUCTION

Every design originates from a base of knowledge and evolves from curiosity—and the more options and experiences that factor into it, the better. Our goal is to design meaning—and feeling—into style. From our very first collaboration, we realized this can happen only when the architecture and the interior design work together seamlessly from day one. That is why we have founded our professional partnership on the mutual understanding that each project needs to have its own visual language, a language that speaks to the project's intent.

The years have taught us both that an intimate familiarity with the world abroad affects decision-making at home. Perhaps this is because we share a love for the contemporary visual arts and for travel in addition to our passion for architecture and interiors. Certainly, the wide lens through which we experience the continuum of history and culture is integral to the way we translate what we see and learn into the houses, apartments, private jets, and other spaces we design, wherever in the world they may be.

Architecture has principles—scale, proportion, balance, harmony—and these apply to interiors as well. But we believe interiors are also about storytelling. We want the spaces we create to incorporate the diverse influences that are intrinsic to each client's way of being in the world. We work to ensure that when the rooms are installed, these qualities are felt and seen, but not blatantly obvious in the way of a first-degree metaphor. This means that each choice we make must be right on its own terms and within the context of the narrative we are constructing.

While either one of us might have the inspiration that establishes this design baseline, we develop it together. We collaborate on the vision for each project, as well as on the spatial planning. Our architecture studio then takes the design in one direction and our interiors studio in another. Even as our focus stays separate, we track the vision together to guarantee the relationship between the two is seamless as we lay out the foundations and layer in the elements of décor to create unique, calm environments that cater to how our clients want to live and feel.

From the first, we set out to create a clear, comprehensible plan organized around defined principles. We lay out each room understanding not only how everything that populates it contributes to the story it tells, but also its role within the entirety of the project. This means art, as well as furniture, fabrics, finishes, architectural details, and accessories. Each project is a brand-new journey. We begin from scratch. We invent the details. The reasoning behind

RIGHT AND OVERLEAF: The cloud-like formations of Ayala Serfaty's *Soma Series* light sculptures and a white-gold leaf finish transform the ceiling into another artistic dimension. Designed for under-shelf lighting, tracks of diminutive fixtures provide an elegant alternative to standard art lights. Ingrid Donat's bronze and leather *Banc Tribal* bench sits beneath Josef Albers's *Homage to the Square*. Perrin & Perrin's glass installation, *Aquatic Life*, splashes across the walls above Maarten Baas's *Carapace* armchair of blackened steel and The Haas Brothers *Daphne Hex* stool.

The living room encompasses two seating areas oriented to capture panoramic views that sweep east and south. Each grouping mixes pieces by some of the twentieth-century's best-known makers with custom designs that enhance the art-above-all point of view. A captivating painting by Ellen Gallagher, the very first work selected for this project, informs the room's elements from form to color palette.

Stationary wall wings separate the living and dining rooms without a more formal closure; these incorporate the soffit profile, as do the details of the cowhide-lined built-in units. Over the dining table, a petal-like arrangement of suede-wrapped panels and delicate descending lights flowers on the ceiling. The library houses an ever-expanding collection of catalogues and art books, as well as comfortable seating and lighting for serious readers. The shelves float on a wall of fabric-wrapped panels set to reveal shadow lines created by a subtle undulation

In the master bedroom, black and gold accents highlight a tonal palette of creams, off-whites, light grays. A fantastic tangle of a lamp by Jean Royère spreads its vines across the hallway; its bold black lines prefigure those in the bedroom's Matisse aquatint. Its curves, as well as Foster's, influence the custom bedroom furnishings. The twin beds in the guest room pick up on the same detail.

It is rare and wonderful to share such trust with clients. When it happens, there's no predicting what art can come of it. And not just the works of art themselves, but the art of furniture, of curating, of placement, and above all, the art of living.

OPPOSITE: Lucio Fontana's *Concetto Spaziale* pops against walls paneled in flat-cut, custom-bleached ash finished with just a hint of charcoal to draw out the grain. Eric Schmitt's *Dragee Console* of patinated bronze and marble makes a strong, functional statement below. OVERLEAF: Ellen Gallagher's *Dew Breaker* dominates one wall of this living room seating area with its bold, watery palette. Shimmering just beneath is Johnny Swing's *Storm King* wave-like bench of welded nickels. Y. Z. Kami's *White Dome I* hangs over Egg Collective's *Howard* sofa facing swivel lounge chairs by Pierre Paulin.

Dan Flavin

OPPOSITE: Giacomo Ravagli's *Barometro Table Lamp 2.1* sits well on a custom bronze-framed onyx end table. ABOVE: The custom coffee table, a puzzle-piece with ceramic tops and blackened steel bases is an homage to the work of midcentury French ceramicist Georges Jouve; Rogan Gregory's *Sculptural Symphysodon disc* rests on the section apart.

RIGHT: In the living room's second seating area, an angled sofa by Christophe Delcourt is perfectly positioned to capture another spectacular city and river view. In the window, Rebecca Warren's bronze *Fascia IV* adds a voluptuous note. A coffee table of kiln-fused glass and cast bronze designed by Stacklab slips neatly into the space. Along the window perimeter are a pair of Hervé Langlais club chairs and an *Ox* chair by Hans Wegner.

On the wall leading into the dining room, Gunther Uecker's *Weibes Feld* suggests waves with a fluid pattern of nails on canvas. Marking the passage between the living and dining areas, a custom screen translates the distinctive curve of the soffit into another interior plane.

OPPOSITE: In the dining room, Warren Platner's classic chairs surround a custom table. On the ceiling, suede upholstered petals frame a shower of lights that shed droplets of illumination onto a glass tabletop cast with a rivulet pattern. OVERLEAF: On the focal wall, Rogan Gregory's unique terrazzo sculpture forms a corolla around George Condo's *Female Composition.*

By the window, Ronan & Erwan Bouroullec's anodized aluminum *Chaines* emphasizes the room's height next to a cast-aluminum console that mimics the color of the city's bluest sky.

BASQUIAT

THE MANOR
WOOD BUILDINGS
LIVING IN TUSCANY
LANDSKIPPING
EQUATOR
DIANE WILLIAMS
FRITZ KAHN
SMALL
Modern Art
NEW YORK CITY LANDMARKS
TRAVELOGUES
100 CONTEMPORARY HOUSES
THE GRAND TOUR

OPPOSITE: On the kitchen wall, Brent Wadden's *Untitled* adds another variation on the recurring black horizontals. Stephane Parmentier's *Cointrin* pendant does the same, making a strong statement over the island. OVERLEAF: The breakfast nook nests into the view. Overhead, a mobile sails above a custom triangular, marble-topped table.

PRECEDING SPREAD: Dan Flavin's *Untitled (To Piet Mondrian)* marks the junction of the gallery and the bedroom corridor. Richard Meier's *Cycladic Circle and Square* sconces light the way into the private quarters. ABOVE AND OPPOSITE: Plaster-finished surfaces add warmth and texture to the master bedroom entry, where Jean Royère's *Liane* fixture winds its way on and off the wall.

RIGHT AND OVERLEAF: A backdrop for Dimorestudio's sconces, the custom headboard reinterprets the curve of the soffit in yet another way. Overhead, Ingo Maurer's *Lil Luxury* ceiling light introduces a touch of gold, repeated by Franck Evennou's set of three nesting tables. A lounge chair and ottoman by Ayala Serfaty nests into one corner; in another, leather club chairs designed by Nina Seirafi huddle around a custom table.

RIGHT: Glazed ceramic vessels insert suggestions of water and sky tones on top of Ludwig & Dominique's oak-topped *Tranche* coffee table. OVERLEAF: Claude Lalanne's *Grains de Café* chair fits perfectly with a custom desk topped by Hervé Van der Straeten's witty table lamp. Brent Wadden's *Untitled* holds the wall with a bold graphic.

Andy Warhol Prints

Andy Warhol Prints

ABOVE AND OPPOSITE: In the second bedroom, custom twin beds dressed in cozy textiles share a single, wall-to-wall headboard and a custom floating nightstand. Yoshitomo Nara's *Jailhouse Kamikaze* floats a dream of sophisticated whimsy above the beds.

JAIL
THE ADVENTURES OF TOM SAWYER
LEWIS CARROLL
ALICE'S ADVENTURES IN WONDERLAND
THE WONDERFUL WIZARD OF OZ

with a modern take on the classic entry stair hall. This leads to a gallery space—we are both life-long collectors—that unfolds into a great room with adjacent living and dining areas. Pocket doors in the gallery and paneled doors in the dining area can completely close off the core with the family room and adjacent kitchen.

Plan in place, the artistic play began. Wood elements stained in tones of ash and cinder reoccur throughout the apartment, establishing a visual rhythm. The darker of the two frames all the transitions, including cased openings in the family room. The interior of those cases incorporates a paler version in wood, or suede or leather, all in the same shade for consistency. We looked at dozens of wood finishes before making a final selection. A pencil-thin reveal traces the vertical and horizontal elements, giving all the surfaces a crafted feel and visually lifting the eight-foot ceilings. Marmorino plaster covers the walls, adding warmth and a feeling of permanence.

Both of us obsess about every single detail, though we approach each from our individual perspective. From the first, we agreed to purchase only pieces we both loved, knowing we would eventually find just the right one. For the most part, we acquired all the pieces we live with now while the design process was underway. The very first material we selected—the stone for the entry hall floor—we discovered underfoot as we were walking along Avenue Montaigne in Paris. We came upon our dining chairs at the Marché aux Puces before we had begun to even think about our dining table. Looking at galleries and attending auctions in Paris, London, and New York, we discovered works of art that appealed to us both, and we introduced each other to our favorite artists.

The background is serene, clean and straightforward because we prefer a calm environment. As collectors, we love furnishings, fabrics, art, and objects with character. These elements can shift the mood of a room in a second. More important, they can change as we do.

For a twist on the classic console-mirror entry pairing, two steel reflectors hang over a slender bronze and parchment table, my homage to Eric Schmitt. Pierre Yovanovitch's *E.T.* table lamp and a Murano glass orb add to the visual conversation.

Simon Baker GEORGE CONDO
JOSEPH DIRAND Interior

PRECEDING SPREAD: Curvaceous pieces—including Afra & Tobia Scarpa's *Soriana* lounge chair and ottoman and a custom sofa with a wide embrace that pays homage to Vladimir Kagan—create a welcoming living area at the far end of the gallery. Sally introduced me to the painter Ron Gorchov, whose *Tournament* focuses this neutral space with a spot of intense color. ABOVE AND OPPOSITE: Chris Wolston's terra-cotta side table and a bamboo lamp with a handmade palm-bark shade and stone base introduce warm, earthy textures, and organic materials into the room's refined, white palette.

ABOVE AND OPPOSITE: We found Ann Veronica Janssens's cast-glass piece, *16 Blue Blocks (405)*, at Art Basel. It draws attention to the custom patinated-steel coffee table. Philip Arctander's cozy lounge chairs contrast with the ceramic *Pebble* table by Armelle Benoit for Pierre Yovanovitch.

PRIVATE

PRECEDING SPREAD: The legs of dining room furniture can compete with each other. Closely inspired by the designs of Martin Szekely, our table features a Corian top with an aluminum honeycomb structure and a plaster base, which allows the black metal frames of the Raoul Guys and Dorothy Schindele chairs to pop. ABOVE AND OPPOSITE: I introduced Sally to the work of George Condo, whose bronze female bust and painting, *Two Figures in Space*, bring so much character to this space.

BENEFITS PLAN

PRECEDING SPREAD: The lack of floor space inspired this custom flip-up console, made of hand-painted resin. Mark Bradford's *Untitled* feels at home above it. OPPOSITE: A pair o panel doors separates the dining room from the family room and adjacent kitchen.

Closing both sets of doors converts the family room into a private space. Two tones of stained oak millwork and soft textiles in a muted palette give the room a warm, cozy feeling. Two of Donald Baechler's *6 Flowers* hang above an end table from Atelier Mathieu Matégot. Next to the sofa, Pierre Yovanovitch's *Little Zou!* table lamp offers a witty comment on a ceramic sculpture by The Haas Brothers.

RICHARD AVEDON PORTRAITS
JEAN-MICHEL BASQUIAT DRAWING
RICK OWENS

Too Young To Die
MICHELE BÖNAN
BEATON

OPPOSITE: On one side of the pocket doors, my built-in desk has a leather-wrapped top for comfort. The chair is twentieth-century classic by Pierre Jeanneret. Antoni Tàpies's *X i ulls* rests against the back wall. Michelangelo Pistoletto's *La Mela Reintegrata* hangs nearby. ABOVE: On the other side of the doorway, a built-in bookcase provides additional storage and display space. A Noguchi lamp behind the sofa offers enough light for reading.

We found Roger Capron's tile coffee table on a walk down the Rue de Seine. Chuck Close's *Phil Fragment* hangs by the entrance to the kitchen. A custom, flush-mount fixture provides soft light overhead. Charlotte Perriand's basic black tripod stool is elemental, bold in form and sized perfectly for a child to use as a step stool up to the taller seating.

PICASSO

RIGHT AND OVERLEAF: With a tone-on-tone palette, layering textures and finishes creates character. The light tones of the palette carry through to the kitchen, where leather-wrapped upper cabinets match the custom-stained oak elements below the honed Alabama white marble counter and backsplash.

RIGHT: When both partners in a marriage are designers, each and every decision involves serious discussion, including such details as whether or not the kitchen should incorporate open shelving. The answer here was yes both for practical reasons—open shelves make reaching easier for the cook—and for aesthetic ones, too. OVERLEAF: In the hall leading to the master suite, a wall of fabric-wrapped closets terminates in a full-length mirror. The reveal detail from downstairs translates upstairs in a variety of ways, including in the closet doors' metal framework. The antique birthing chair from Sally's London house feels right at home here. Raoul Guys's midcentury rattan and metal chair slips neatly into one of the bedroom corners.

PRECEDING SPREAD, ABOVE, AND OPPOSITE: The color palette of the master suite takes its cues from the family room. Marmorino plaster walls envelope the room with warmth. A soft, durable suede wraps the headboard. An oddly shaped box found at the Chanel boutique in London inspired the design of the nightstands. Ceramic sconces cast a soft glow. Robert Greene's three-panel *James* hangs above the bed.

In the master bath, a mirrored door expands the space. Light fixtures inserted into the stonework cast a flattering glow. The honed Carrara marble that lines all the surfaces gives the space a soft, timeless feel.

MODERN HISTORY

All design emerges from the point-counterpoint of relationships: dark and light, straight and curved, hard and soft, historic and modern, and so on. The interiors of this Tribeca loft celebrate the idea of contrast, largely because the client, a real estate developer who loves art, design, and all things beautiful, does too. He has a passion for the neighborhood's collage of cobblestone streets, nineteenth-century manufacturing structures, twenty-first-century superscrapers, and more—an architectural melting pot from Manhattan's settled start to now. He admires this landmark building, an 1882 bookbindery by noted architect Charles C. Haight, which tells a romantic tale of the past through soaring ceilings, exposed beams, arched windows, and views of historic structures.

The entry sets the stage for everything to come, introducing a specific idea of person and place full-on through the selection of furnishings, finishes, objects, and art. It features some elements expected of Tribeca, including industrial metal sheets that carry forward the light industry of the area's past and linen-wrapped wall and ceiling panels set in a pattern that alludes to the cobblestone streets below. There are also clear artistic references—to Mondrian, specifically—in the repeated, dark framing device and red suede panels. A Jean Dubuffet print and Chris Wolston's textured metal pieces offset any hints of angular rigidity.

Two living areas range symmetrically off a central axis that leads straight to an arched window, the perfect crown for the client's Fernando Botero sculpture. In one, an arresting painting by Shepard Fairey hangs over a luxe, velvet-covered sofa. This work feels like a controlled explosion of curves and sharp lines; it is also a happy, two-dimensional exclamation

RIGHT AND OVERLEAF: This client, an art collector and design lover, has a deep feel for New York's rhythms and history. Mondrian-inspired geometries in the entry—a kind of lower Broadway boogie-woogie—make that clear from the start. Bronze, red suede, linen, and wood introduce the interior's language of materials and textures. Dubuffet's *Lion Heraldique* captures the spirit (and the color palette). Jason Koharik's light fixture provides a fractal of shimmer overhead. Chris Wolston's sandcast aluminum stool and chair add art, craft, and unexpected texture to the mix.

Dan Flavin The Complete Lights, 1961–1996
Alberto Giacometti

IMPERIAL
Glory
EAMES

PRECEDING SPREAD, ABOVE, AND OPPOSITE: A central axis from the front door divides the main space into two distinct living areas. Linking them is Botero's *Girl*, installed under an arched window. The Botero stands next to India Mahdavi's aptly named (and shaped) *Botero* swivel chairs. Precisely positioned to balance the elevation, Shepard Fairey's *Imperial Glory* hangs over a custom velvet-covered sofa, infusing the space with movement and color.

Jean Royère
Jean Royère

RIGHT AND OVERLEAF: In the dining room, a custom pedestal table features an onyx top. Its abstracted Lazy Susan core echoes the natural order of the ranunculus images captured in Christopher Beane's brilliantly colored photographs. Subtle elements of patinated brass enhance black lacquer dining chairs with velvet upholstery. Sconces by Patrick Naggar flank a buffet topped by Yves Hayat's *Les Icônes Sont Fatiguées*; Louise Nevelson's *Double Imagery (2175B)* animates the wall above.

Art helps bring every area of the loft to life, including the kitchen, where bold pieces by Pat Steir introduce visual spice. Alexander Lamont's *Peking Concubine Vase, Imperial Yellow* provides a colorful splash to the island.

RIGHT AND OVERLEAF: In the master bedroom, the Mondrian-inspired geometry resurfaces in a palette of strié plaster and wall-mounted panels of suede, sapele mahogany, and other materials. David Alexander's bedside pendants contribute to the romance. Roger Capron's tile-topped coffee table is a counterpoint to the rug pattern. In one corner, Franco Albini's classic lounge chair abuts a dresser found on a stroll down the Pimlico Road.

Jean Royère

OLD WORLD MEETS MODERN

Every project begins as a tabula rasa. The challenge is twofold. First is the process of discovering how the clients want to live and what emotions they want their rooms to evoke. Then comes the challenge of developing a unique design language for their material expression. This sophisticated New York-based couple travels internationally on business all the time. They own a villa in Italy. They spend a considerable amount of time in Asia. For their new home base in New York, they wanted this apartment in the West Village to reflect what they love about those places. What captivates them about their Italian villa is its texture, light, and old-world feel. The appeal of Asian design is its characteristic strength, delicacy, and powerful simplicity.

It is one thing to reflect diverse influences. It is another to create living spaces that, when complete, are coherent and replete with these qualities in a subtle way. For a multi-layered design that goes beyond a first-degree metaphor, every detail has to serve its own purpose—and that of the overall narrative. Here, research into European and Asian influences inspires every single element. Carefully collected pieces of furniture, art, and objects do not just plant these references into the rooms; they support and enhance the larger design story and its underlying values.

The entry sequence introduces the architectural spirit, language, and palette, ensuring that as the rooms unfold, they are understood. In the foyer, Jerusalem limestone pavers with textured edges, walls of troweled plaster, and plaster ceilings with strapwork call to mind a Tuscan villa, but in a streamlined, New York way. There is romance, a hint of the old world, and a true play of light because daylight dances through every area of this apartment from dawn to dusk. The furniture and artwork start to tell the tale of the owners' travels.

In the entry, Jerusalem stone floors and troweled plaster walls evoke the old-world textures of the owners' much-loved Italian villa. The stone base detail tracks across the doors and runs throughout, a subtle, unifying element. The settee is a reference to their romance with Asia. Ronnie Tjampitjinpa's *Untitled* adds bold color.

The stone captures the daylight as it moves and changes in an inviting way. The finishes and details add warmth and layers of reference both to their villa and to Asian design in a New York mode. Deliberate joint lines within the strapwork contribute to the modern feeling. Cased stone openings frame the spaces and beckon people in.

With traditional, modern, and vernacular elements of various periods and origins, the living room reflects the clients' lifestyle. Wood screening allows them to close off and open the adjoining spaces. A traditional Aubusson carpet gives the room a grounding of subtle color.

MIES

For definition and a sense of invitation, limestone-cased openings frame the spaces that unfold off the foyer. Sliding wood screens rather than fixed walls divide the living room, dining room, and study. The clients can open each room into the others at will, or close areas off for intimacy and privacy. The idea for the screens and their pragmatic use come from elements of Asian architecture, as do the pronounced coffered ceilings.

Conveying even more about the couple, simple modern chairs surround a traditional Italian table in the dining room, where a red-lacquer, Asian-style cabinet folds in an influence from the other side of the globe. In the living room, an Aubusson carpet gives a traditional foundation to modern furnishings. It also weaves in the blue and orange tones that, in various shades and intensities, thread a connection through the spaces. Because these two are serious readers—every photo they showed us was cluttered with books—we designed bookcases throughout.

The design of the kitchen mattered to them greatly. They wanted it to be a beautiful space suited for entertaining, but an area that they could also sequester from the rest of the apartment. They specifically asked for a unique stove that would look like a piece of industrial sculpture and serve as a focal point. Sliding, ribbed wood doors at the entry, which pick up on the screen motif, can close off the room when desired. A long marble counter doubles as a buffet. The cabinets incorporate an undulating door system wrapped in treated linen that ties in seamlessly with the interior's other architectural details.

The architecture of the master bedroom posed a challenge to furniture placement because there was no wall space for a headboard. Floating the bed in the center solved the problem. European influences merge with Asian simplicity in the master bath—and serenity reigns.

OPPOSITE: Architectural and concealed lighting offer both practicality and great flexibility for changing the mood of each room. Cut into the ceiling, trimless downlights virtually disappear. A velvet-covered daybed by Mathieu Matégot completes the living room seating. OVERLEAF: In the dining room, a traditional Italian table surrounded by simple modern chairs, Asian-style red-lacquer buffet, troweled plaster walls and ceiling, and open-cut wood floors combine in a unified vision of modern global reach with hints of the old world. Adjusting the screens shifts the focus within the space; moving both to the center of the opening reveals views into the adjacent study.

PIANO
COBRA
Magritte

In his study, custom built-in shelving units house an extensive collection of books. Robert Mangold's *Double Square Frame I* hangs over the sofa. George Nakashima's grass-seated wood chair evokes the master craftsman's reverence for natural materials and simplicity.

LORE OF RUNNING
THE POWER BROKER
LEAN IN
STALIN
MAO
Eric Schmitt
DESIGN BROOKLYN
IVÁN NAVARRO
RENZO PIANO

The desk in his study is the one piece the couple brought with them. He assembled it from two old wood doors mounted on a trestle base. Faded remnants of blue paint complement the shades of blue in the carpet and on the storage system.

OPPOSITE: Ribbed closet doors echo the slatwork of the screens, a vivid, vertical blue counterpoint to the low, horizontal of the blue cabinets behind the desk. OVERLEAF: Because this couple entertains, they specifically requested a showplace for the kitchen with a long counter to serve as a buffet. The custom hood works as a pragmatic sculptural statement.

An edge detail on the countertop works as a containment device. Wrapped in treated linen for protection and easy maintenance, the undulating door system picks up on the texture of the screens and hides most of the kitchen's working elements, including the refrigerator.

OPPOSITE: The kitchen includes a space for more casual, intimate meals. Various shades of blue and gray reoccur throughout, from the living room all the way through to the kitchen and master suite. The same is true for the plaster walls and Jerusalem stone floor. OVERLEAF: A linen-wrapped wall of closets with beveled door details adds texture, character, and color to the serene master bedroom. Custom doors incorporate references to Asian architecture, including the metal detailing.

Given two window walls, a wall of closets, and a wall with central doors, the best option for positioning the bed was to float it within the room. The back of the headboard incorporates a deep shelf that can function as a desktop; the nightstands pull out for additional storage.

OPPOSITE: The closets wrap around into a hall that leads to the master bath. With a wall of glass-fronted closets and a mirrored door at one end, this space feels light and serene. OVERLEAF: The master bath incorporates Asian references to create a spirit of calm and softness. The custom his-and-hers vanity intentionally resembles a piece of furniture rather than a more predictable built-in. A side reveal in the shower creates handy storage space that is in keeping with overall simplicity of the design.

IN THE CLOUDS

Taste is an aesthetic point of view. Occasionally, it can be broad enough to embrace what feels like a major disconnect. This couple, both fashion designers, love the atmosphere of Soho House New York, the Manhattan outpost of the international private club, and Scandinavian design with equal passion—a major conflict, at least on the surface. Soho House is all clubby warmth, full of library-like, dark collected spaces, each with a different spirit. Scandinavian design is all clean lines, authentic materials, crafted with a form-follows-function purposefulness. But there is a deeper truth that drove the design of this three-bedroom glass house perched high in Herzog & de Meuron's cantilevered Tribeca superscraper. For this couple, who met as students at Parsons School of Design, Soho House feels familiar, a home away from home to meet friends and share ongoing conversations about life. They similarly prize Scandinavian design for its lightness of being, its comfort, and its use of natural materials.

The two travel often and widely. They know and care about real furniture. They prefer rooms that feel collected, like those at Soho House. For these reasons, it made sense to broaden the net beyond the canon of twentieth-century Swedish, Danish, and Finnish pieces and bring in works of contemporary designers from around the globe who embody the same characteristics, tones, and values. The idea of a light palette—true to the Scandinavian aesthetic—makes perfect sense for rooms amid the clouds.

All the spaces have unusual floor plates with odd angles and interior columns, which encouraged a Soho House-like organization of settings with different moods within a predominantly open plan. The entry sets the stage with art, carefully selected midcentury furnishings and lighting, and a custom cantilevered console that alludes to the individual elements of the

To establish the Scandinavian design meets Soho House aesthetic, the entry incorporates clean-lined pieces from various countries and eras, such as Carlo Hauner's wrought-iron-framed bench for Forma, Brazil; Charlotte Perriand's black enamel sconces; the midcentury ceramic table lamp by Louis Giraud; and a metal-framed chair manufactured by Ahrend in the Netherlands, a fortuitous find at a flea market in London.

building's stacked construction. The large living room encompasses two zones: the primary one feels more open; the secondary, more intimate. In the main area, a Royère chair sits with classic designs by Hans Wegner, Poul Kjaerholm, and Charlotte Perriand. Contemporary and custom pieces figure into this mix as well. Two Danish chairs by Jørgen and Nanna Ditzel and a custom coffee table, among other furnishings, beckon in the more intimate area. Two different versions of a custom sofa—one with arms for coziness, the other armless to welcome large groups without blocking the view, and both upholstered in the same fabric—tie the two areas together. The living area also embraces another adjacent space—formerly a bedroom—arranged for gathering, lounging, or work. It incorporates a daybed by Jean Prouvé and a Serge Mouille lamp—discovered side-by-side in Paris and installed the same way here—plus a relaxed, comfortable chair and a table that propped-up feet will not harm. With a darker palette, this area feels like a private retreat.

They entertain, so the custom dining table can extend to accommodate friends and family. A woven, basket-like fixture hangs overhead, softening the hard edges of the city beyond the windows. A game table and chairs by Gio Ponti fit neatly into one of the unusual nooks created by the apartment's irregular floor plate. A cantilevered vanity adds interest to the hallway leading to to the master bedroom. Even here, there are multiple areas to sit, to read, and to contemplate the view.

The various textures, the consistent wood tones, the light palette, and the art marry a broad spectrum of design into a harmonious aesthetic—and a single point of view.

OPPOSITE: Herzog & de Meuron's superscraper at 56 Leonard Street is known as the Jenga Tower after the Japanese stacking game. This stair-step plan of the condominium floors ensures that every room has a corner or balcony that juts into the sky. OVERLEAF: Above the entry hall console, the blues of Kate Shepherd's *White Boat, Deep Sea, Dented Cloud* brings the colors of the sky-scape deep into the interior. The pure geometry of Kelly Lamb's *Unique Small Gem Platter* harks back to midcentury Nordic ceramics. At the other end of the entry hall, a watercolor by Gabriel Vormstein provides a focal point. The tonal rug designed by Maddalena Forcella nods to midcentury Swedish ryas.

VICTORIA HAGAN

RIGHT: With upholstered pieces, interesting textures, and a palette of whites and off-whites straight from the clouds, the main living area feels like a welcoming island in the sky. A custom sofa, an armchair by Jean Royère, Hans Wegner's *Papa Bear* wing chair, and Poul Kjaerholm's *1956 PK-61* coffee table create an inviting seating group.

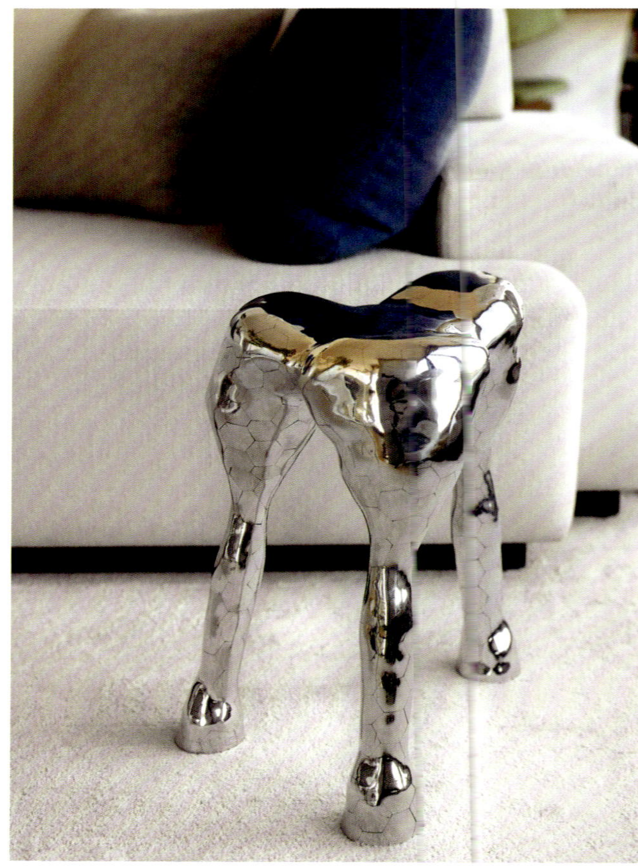

ABOVE: The Haas Brothers' *Jax* porcelain "sea urchin" and three-legged aluminum stool layer in the wit of contemporary design. OPPOSITE: A game table and chairs by Gio Ponti occupy a corner with a remarkable view. One of Andrew Neyer's fixtures extends out from the column to light the table top.

PRECEDING SPREAD: The sleek white kitchen offers a bright, convenient workspace and a seamless backdrop for the black island and adjacent dining area. The stools introduce a Danish influence. OPPOSITE: Doug Johnston's *4H Light Sculpture* of coiled cotton and nylon cord lends a softening element over the custom extending table and Edward Wormley chairs. Kiki Smith's *Dandelions* series rests along the counter. A ceramic vase by Lee Hun Chung holds the flowers.

The custom, armed sofa, custom coffee table, and pair of Jørgen and Nanna Ditzel's armchairs in the secondary living area relate closely to the furnishings in the main living space, but the grouping has a more intimate feel. Martha Sturdy's resin *Chief Open Cube* doubles as an end table and book storage. Blue and indigo accents tie the interior to the exterior. The floor lamp with two different shades is by midcentury Swedish designer Greta Magnusson Grossman for Ralph O. Smith.

IVÁN NAVARRO
SKYSCRAPERS

LEFT AND OVERLEAF: A darker palette defines the den area, where a Jean Prouvé daybed sits below Dubuffet's *Evocations*. The lounge chair is a midcentury design by Folke Ohlsson for Fritz Hansen. Fixtures by Serge Mouille provide reading light. Cody Hoyt's patterned ceramic vessel *Curved Walls (Twisted Rim)* and Judy Engel's *Ceramic Ball Sculpture* fit naturally into the mix. A hide pillow boosts the play of textures with another organic element.

A passion for
JEAN PROUVÉ
From furniture to architecture
The Laurence
A passion for Jean Prouvé
The Laurence and Patrick Seguin collection
Pinacoteca Giovanni e Marella Agnelli
Galerie Patrick Seguin
PAUL VAN DE KOOI

Scandinavian design is all about the directness of form, authentic materials and textures, and honest craftsmanship. Hans Wegner's *Mama Bear* chair epitomizes the ethic. The resin side table, a contemporary piece, shows a similar spirit, as does The Haas Brothers' hand-thrown vessel, *Father with Peacock Fade Accretion.*

The layout of the master bath makes the most of the spectacular panoramic views.

FAMILY OASIS

Every New Yorker craves some kind of retreat from the pace of the city. What this means in design terms is a matter of perspective, though, as the light, open spaces that feel life-enhancing to one person may have the opposite effect on another. These clients—a couple with two young daughters—love to retreat and relax at home with family and friends. Immersed daily in the Manhattan maelstrom, they have always placed a high priority on living spaces that transport them out of the chaos when they cross the threshold. For this family, calm comes from brightness, order, and control. There is more to their serenity than simplicity and a pale palette, though. Balancing all the comforts is one thing. Expressing personality with finishes, textures, furnishings, details, and art is another.

The entry gives the first hints of the forceful subtleties to come. A modern version of historically inspired moldings frames plaster walls, a subtle defining feature that activates the contained space. A floor of pale and paler tones of stone in a controlled, orderly pattern starts to develop a private language of relaxed and understated excitement. The painting is also very inviting, a bright abstraction of light by Jessica Dickinson. A millwork partial wall screens and divides the entry from the inner rooms; it doubles as a backdrop for the entry's mirror and console and, on the other side, houses the bar.

The living room is airy comfort—a mix of large, contemporary pieces with some twentieth-century design classics. A palette of light neutrals and pale pastels and a mix of super-soft fabrics and buttery leathers sets a relaxed enveloping mood. A triptych over the sofa by Robert Greene infuses the room with more intense versions of the same soft shades. The overhead lighting is key: 3-by-3-inch fixtures create pools of downlight and angle to highlight the art.

A patterned stone entry floor with hints of tradition begins to establish elements of the light, calm, orderly design language used throughout. A built-in floor-to-ceiling partial wall element sets up a contemporary take on the classic foyer console/mirror arrangement; it evolved as a response to a question about whether or not to block the view of the interior from the front door. A luminous painting by Jessica Dickinson adds in another layer of light.

The dining area is on the other side of the entry divider wall. Pared back to the most sensual lines and sculptural curves, it centers on a custom table that expands for larger gatherings and a suite of Eero Saarinen's upholstered side chairs that bring the yin to the table base's yang. The craquelure of the table's lacquered eggshell top bears a faint echo of the patterned entry hall floor.

The powder room takes the lightness of being to another level with a mix of onyx elements, mirror, and mother-of-pearl finishes. In the open kitchen, opalescent glass cabinets, both practical and pretty, reflect light in a kaleidoscope of shifting pastels. Glass countertops and a marble backsplash add more pragmatic elements of shine. Carefully placed wood surfaces ensure that the room stays warm and welcoming.

The den/family room/home office takes a cozy, darker turn. A sofa large enough for the whole family lines one wall. On another, a built-in cabinet houses his leather-topped desk. Ceilings finished with Venetian plaster add polish overhead. A metal channel detail brings architectural order to the fabric-paneled walls. The master bedroom feels like the Jessica Dickinson painting in the entrance in three dimensions: full of light, soft around the edges. The master bath follows suit. Lined in Bianco Neve marble, it, too, has a quiet glow.

In terms of architectural details, this interior is clean and seamless. Understated crown moldings and baseboards respect the traditional design values of the Upper East Side. Within that framework, a modern point of view emerges through furnishings and art.

The living room furniture is large scale but light, with a mix of deep, comfortable, contemporary upholstered pieces and a few modern classics. Placed with ample breathing room, the seating beckons in a relaxed way. The palette is soft and light, a serene contrast to the world outside the apartment doors. A triptych by Robert Greene folds in more saturated hues.

Just as color and light make profound contributions to a room's mood, materials and textures have the same impact on its feeling. The client wanted these interiors to be calm, light, and inviting. Leather, cashmere, steel, and soft, but robust wools in pale hues are intrinsic to achieving that.

ABOVE AND OPPOSITE: Contrasting textures bring sensuality and intimacy to the dining area. The custom table expands for larger groups. The shape of the base speaks nicely to the lines of the Saarinen-designed side chairs. The table top is finished with lacquered eggshells. OVERLEAF: The interior-facing side of the built-in houses a bar. Venetian plaster adds a subtle reflective quality to the walls of the hallway leading to the bedrooms.

A subtle glow emanates from the powder room's onyx surfaces. A traditional bevel translates the molding details into the onyx wall, sink, and counter; the design integrates an inset mirror to expand the space. Mother of pearl shimmers on the walls. OVERLEAF: In the open kitchen, easy-to-clean opalescent-glass cabinets reflect the surrounding pastels; the colors dance across the surfaces throughout the day in a way that's subtle, pretty, and very inviting. Glass countertops enhance the effect. The marble behind the sink ties into the shifting colors of the glass, while the wood floor and island base add warmth. Peter Combe's *Hell, Yes* hangs in the kitchen, injecting a positive note.

yes

HADID

PRECEDING SPREAD: This space serves as a den, a media room, and his office. A cozy custom sofa is large enough so that all four family members can sit togethe and watch TV. ABOVE AND OPPOSITE: A cantilevered built-in case piece houses his leather-topped desk on one wall. Venetian plaster on the ceiling subtly transforms the quality of light in the room.

In the den, the different textiles and textures create a warm environment, enhanced by the darker palette. A metal channel detail adds architectural definition and a tailored touch to the fabric-wrapped wall panels that dampen sound.

Soft and flowing with light, the master bedroom seems to bring the Dickinson painting in the entry hall into three dimensions. The many shades of creams and whites give this room a quiet energy as the light changes throughout the day. A silk rug adds a shimmer and softness underfoot. Fabric-wrapped walls add to the effect. The plaid on the lounge chairs picks up a pattern used elsewhere in the interior.

A glowing white space, the master bath is covered in Bianco Neve marble apart from some highlighted details. A chair by Piero Fornasetti introduces a bold design note and a bracing comment on the palette.

The Haas Brothers' *Teddy Bear* provides a witty focal point at the turning point of a hall outside the master bedroom. Finished in Venetian plaster, the walls radiate a subtle yet energetic luminosity.

POWER PENTHOUSE

Every New Yorker, transplant or native, lives out a unique New York story. This bachelor, a London-based asset manager, could not have been clearer about his own vision—and the ultimate glass penthouse that he imagined as its perfect setting. He found the space of his dreams atop a crystal-shaped tower on East 57th Street. Surrounded by sky, he asked for rich, dark spaces. Beyond that, he wanted to be surprised. In looking for another detail beyond the palette to tether the design to his identity, the stock ticker came to mind; hence the banding detail that tracks throughout.

Gutting the entire space to the concrete structure allowed for a complete reinvention. Three bedrooms became two. An inconveniently located, closed-off kitchen became well positioned and open. Generous new pathways enhanced circulation around enlarged living spaces. A newly created sequence of entry introduced a syncopated rhythm of volumes to the processional spaces. In the elevator lobby, lustrous, dark materials—smoked mirrors, bronzed steel, and glass—create a dramatic first impression and a memorable last look; the banding detail makes quite an entrance here as leather straps wrap lacquer panels. In the adjacent, newly created foyer, huge slabs of Grigio Carnico marble cover soaring walls; a dropped glass ceiling and glass flooring seem to compress the volume, playing with spatial perception. The horizontal banding, here in metal, reinforces the proportions, and embossed suede panels in a deep shade of merlot layer in a rich, tactile element that is both soft and masculine.

The main living areas, with floors of Negro Marquina marble, seem to expand upward from the foyer into a triangular volume sheathed in 14-foot glass walls. In a razor-sharp corner that points to Central Park, a built-in daybed appears to float out over the city. Round concrete columns help define the individual areas. The living room riffs on masculine themes, with a

OPPOSITE AND OVERLEAF: The foyer of this New York bachelor pad sets the stage for the owner's preferred rich, dark palette, composed of Grigio Carnico marble, smoked mirrors, bronzed steel, embossed suede, and glass surfaces. A *Cabbage* chair by the Japanese designer Nendo adds a softer touch of cool to the space. Embossed suede panels bring more richness and the contrast of a sensuous tactile element. The suede rolls into the powder room, where a single slab of Kenya Black marble forms the sink and counter.

MAXIMALISM
DARING CREATIVITY

deep club chair by Jean Royère, large yet precisely tailored sofas, and, among other occasional pieces, two side tables by Eric Schmitt—one glass-topped, the other, sleek and understated—found in Paris. A pair of crafted, steel, glass, and blackened bronze architectural coffee tables help tame the dimensions.

The media room is darker, cozy and embracing, with a fabric-paneled wall that conceals the TV. Architectural built-ins sheathed in custom stained Koto panels give character to the vertical surfaces. A Campana Brothers chair offers high design, as do a pair of vintage *Lady* chairs by Marco Zanuso, Gary Magakis's *Stacked Low Table*, and Charles Haupt's *Num Num Branch II*.

In the dining area, a feature wall of custom stained-and-polished woodwork creates a sleek backdrop for vintage Lucite chairs and a custom dining table. With a small reveal at the bottom, the table's base seems to levitate slightly; a dark tint gives the glass top a distinctive glamour.

In the master bedroom, everything is built in, and the luxe materials take on an even more sumptuous feel. A particularly beautiful Blue de Savoie marble lines the master bath. Thassos marble sheathes the tub, which is built into a difficult corner. All the design details converge in the guest bedroom, including the reveal that tracks all the way through from the entrance into the guest bathroom. A work by Jacob Hashimoto animates the space above the bed. In a feat of engineering, a cantilevered stone desk slips through a glass panel and into the guest bath.

Treated like works of art, the materials and details capture the eye and the imagination. Even better, they tell another story at night.

PRECEDING SPREAD: Glass curtain walls meet in a sharp angle in the triangular living room, creating some unusual spatial issues. A lounge area with a daybed built into the tip of the angle feels as if it's floating over the city. The furnishings play hard against soft and curves against straight lines. Fran Taubman's glass-topped steel plate and blackened-bronze plate coffee tables echo the architectural rigor within and in the skyline beyond. A square concrete wall slab—evocatively screened from floor-to-ceiling with backlit metal banding—bridges the living and media rooms. OPPOSITE: Paired with a red glass-topped table by Eric Schmitt, Jean Royère's *Polar Bear* chair is poised to take advantage of the view.

PRECEDING SPREAD: In the media room the fabric-wrapped panel that conceals the TV also provides a backdrop for *Blind Land (Green Mirror)* by Teresita Fernández. A low, built-in cabinet in custom Koto panels incorporates a bronzed steel shelf that, with the Negro Marquina floor, layers in the entry's materials. Gary Magakis's *Stacked Low Table* gives this space its center of gravity. Charles Haupt's *Num Num Branch II* introduces a sly reference to nature. Fernando and Humberto Campana's *Bolotas* armchair injects a burst of strong color and texture. ABOVE AND OPPOSITE: Marco Zanuso's *Lady* chairs, the Serge Mouille lamp, and Eric Schmitt's bronze side table subtly reflect each other's curves.

PRECEDING SPREAD: The dining area combines Lucite, chrome, bronzed steel, tinted glass, and custom-stained, highly polished Koto panels in a powerfully sensuous tableau. Jeff Messerschmidt's Lucite *Pipe Line II* chairs bring their 1980s style to the glamorous custom table. OPPOSITE: In the kitchen, 3-by-6-foot Negro Marquina slabs cover the floor and the island. Countertops and window cabinet tops of Wallace Creek limestone provide contrast. All the lights are recessed into the lacquered ceiling. Glass covers the cabinet doors and backsplash. Marino Di Teana's *Dynamique au Depart* sits on the island; Maté Lapierre's bronze rests by the window.

PRECEDING SPREAD: The master bedroom incorporates built-ins of eucalyptus with bronzed steel and satin nickel pulls and accents of Blue de Savoie marble. Sconces found in a flea market outside Paris climb the leather-detailed, fabric-covered wall behind the bed. OPPOSITE: In the bedroom workspace, a chair designed by Michel Dufet in the 1930s reintroduces the banding detail next to a custom desk and an Eric Schmitt lamp. OVERLEAF: By the window, Carol Egan's *Sculptural Carved Chair* sits next to Friedemann Buehler's *Limed Ashwood* vase.

AMERICAN ORIGINALS WILLIAM ABRANOWICZ
de GRISOGONO
ASSOULINE
LICHTENSTEIN POSTERS
PRESTEL

Lined in Blue de Savoie marble and too beautiful to sequester behind doors, the master bath remains open to view from the master bedroom. The vanity brings in the eucalyptus from the bedroom. A built-in tub sheathed in Thassos marble fits into the room's sharp corner and embraces the view.

A Jacob Hashimoto wall collage adds a blast of color, pattern, and texture to the guest bedroom. Different nightstands flank the bed: one, a pair of custom nesting tables adds an understated curve to soften the room's basic geometry.

PRECEDING SPREAD, LEFT: An electrified glass panel that connects the guest bed and bath becomes a privacy screen when turned on. A darker Fior di Bosco marble sheathes the Thassos-lined bath, which incorporates a seat for steaming. PRECEDING SPREAD, RIGHT: A reveal detail first introduced in the foyer proceeds all the way through the apartment and into the wall panel arrangement in the guest bedroom. Mark de la Vega's *Giac* chair pulls up to the guest bedroom's Thassos desktop, which slides from the bedroom through into the en suite bath on the other side of the glass panel. An inset mirror conceals the TV. OPPOSITE: Pocketing doors enclose the tub when the guest prefers to shower. The stool is by Floris Wubben.

OPPOSITE: The wine bar takes in the view at night, when the apartment becomes a different kind of showplace. A painting by Julian Stanczak stands in front of the view. Rogan Gregory's *Fertility Form* lamp lends a touch of the feminine. A vase by Eric Astoul provides an earthy, sculptural contrast. OVERLEAF: With leather strapping around black lacquer panels, and bronzed steel reveals, the elevator hall encapsulates the client's ideal of Gotham City. Custom columnar light strips influenced by the work of Dan Flavin layer in an artistic reference and expand on the idea of craft. Marc Bankowsky's *Pieds de Bouc* stool adds softness and wit to the space's edgy, masculine attitude.

PH

THOMAS HICKEY

My curiosity about architecture developed when I was a child. While stationed overseas, my parents made it a point to visit historic sites wherever we happened to be. We toured through Europe's many classical styles, the vast geometries and engineering feats of Turkey's Ottoman-influenced structures, and the naturalistic tendencies celebrated by traditional Korean buildings. Through these excursions, I discovered the notion that the worlds we create can, and often do, embody the distinctive spirit that makes each culture unique.

Seeing images of Fallingwater after we moved back to the United States confirmed my growing passion. I marveled at the way Frank Lloyd Wright's design embraced the conditions of its site, appearing to hover over the waterfall. The simplicity of Wright's architectural gesture and complexity of the engineering expressed in modern terms what I had learned from all the historic buildings I had seen while traveling with my family. As we settled into a part of Virginia that celebrated its colonial roots, my enthusiasm for modern design continued to grow, so much so that it drove my choice of colleges.

At the University of Kentucky, José Oubrerie, the dean of the architecture school and a protégé of Le Corbusier, exposed me to a whole new world. One of the benefits of Kentucky's curriculum was its semester-abroad program in Venice. In those few months there, we traveled everywhere, saw everything, and studied architectural and art history in great depth and detail. Studying under Leonardo Ricci, a renowned Italian architect who engrained in his students the tripartite principle of model, structure, form, I learned to see the underlying logic of the architecture, object, or space. From then on, design's organizational systems have fascinated me. Today, a version of Ricci's three-part procedure—research, design, execution—serves as a foundational philosophy for our practice.

Pursuing my master's degree at Columbia University, I was a graduate teaching assistant. Degree in hand, I became an assistant professor of architecture in the Barnard Columbia undergraduate architecture program and a faculty member at Parsons School of Design, teaching interior design.

I joined Robert A.M. Stern Architects to learn more about high-end residential architecture—I have always related better to the way one touches a doorknob than to a monument or skyscraper—and I continued to teach. In these years, I gradually realized that the most robust design solutions come when architecture and interiors go hand in hand.

Edward and I met in one of my interior design studios at Parsons. Early on, we realized that we shared a vision about what living spaces should be, and can be at their best. By his graduation, we had embarked together on the exciting venture that has evolved into GRADE New York.

From the outset, we have strived to create spaces that are grounded in historical precedents, take cues from their context, and have a view to the future. On each project, our architecture and interior design teams work closely together from concept through design development in pursuit of the most cohesive solutions.

EDWARD YEDID

My passion for design, art, and travel traces back to my parents. My father, a fantastically cultured man, loved everything to do with the visual arts and languages. He had grown up in Beirut, Lebanon, moved to New York to continue his banking career, and met and married my mother, an exceptional cook and hostess with a great eye for design. My earliest memories marry all these influences together: traveling with my parents all over Europe, staying in wonderful places, meeting the people from around the globe they regularly entertained at our home, who always came bearing gifts, including the blocks and Legos that obsessed me as a young child. At age nine, my mother let me design my bedroom. All modern lines, charcoal and heather gray fabrics mixed with pops of chartreuse and the bed deliberately angled to maximize the view—it felt very cool then. Today, it seems like a sign of everything to come.

In college, I began to study business, first at Boston University and then at New York University. Looking for more, I moved to Paris with my best friend. As we traveled here and there, I started to fall in love with all things European, especially design and architecture. Six months later, I came home. Knowing by then I wanted to be an interior designer, I immediately enrolled at Parsons. Noel JeFrey, a celebrated interior designer and father of a close friend, gave me a life-changing opportunity in his office. This introduced me to the world of high-end design and many of the gifted artisans we still work with today. In my first year at Parsons, I worked during the day and took classes in the evenings. Thomas, one of my studio professors, introduced me to the work of Louis Kahn and Le Corbusier, which prompted an exploration of the incredibly rich history of twentieth-century design innovation that continues to this day. Soon enough, I was sleeping, breathing, and had begun collecting all things design, art, and furniture. I also continued traveling to Europe as often as possible.

As I was finishing school, friends started asking me to do small interiors projects. Wanting to create at the highest level, and convinced that architecture was critical to the equation, I approached Thomas, who had recently launched GRADE Architecture, about working together in some capacity. We both believed that to produce the best solutions, we should integrate interior design and architecture from the outset. The next fall, we launched GRADE New York. It slowly grew, as did our understanding of each other's values and our goals for our new venture. The relationship we have developed in the years since we began our collaboration has enriched our lives—and our approach to design—so profoundly,

Every time I find myself in Paris, London (my wife, Sally's, home), and the many other parts of the world she and I travel to each year, I am filled with inspiration. Visiting art and design fairs, museums, and the many gallerists, dealers, auction houses, and artisans we work with, I learn so much. With each trip, I find myself falling in love with design, art, and furniture all over again. This obsession with beauty—and with creating contemporary beauty for living—fuels everything we do at GRADE. From the vision through the space planning to the finishes, furnishings, fabrics, accessories, and each carefully selected work of art, this is what I work to bring to the uniquely personal interiors we design.

ACKNOWLEDGMENTS

In design, the truth is that the one always comes from the many. Each day at GRADE reminds us that we could not do what we do alone. Shepherding a project from conception to completion requires so many different skills and talents, to say nothing of experience and sheer determination. We are grateful to all who have been involved with our company and its growth from day one, whether the role you have played in helping us has been small or large.

To our clients, thank you for your support and trust. You inspire us to do our best for you as we continue to learn from you on every project.

Collaboration is the essence of every design practice. We feel especially fortunate in our GRADE team. Their passion, commitment, loyalty, and professionalism contribute beyond measure to every project. Perhaps even more important, they make work a pleasure.

To all the vendors, artisans, contractors who help us design, engineer, and build our designs, thank you for making our dreams come true.

To Elizabeth White and the entire team at The Monacelli Press, our appreciation is beyond measure for your support and belief in our work and this book.

Jill Cohen, there is no one like you. Thank you for your expertise, vision, and enthusiasm—and for pulling together an incredible team to help champion our work onto these pages.

Richard Powers, we marvel at the way you, working with the stylist Anita Sarsidi, have captured the spirit of our spaces in your photographs. We cannot thank you both enough. William Abranowicz, we are also grateful for the contribution your artist's eye and camera make to these pages.

Doug Turshen and Steve Turner, your skill at presenting the three dimensional in two dimensions is beyond compare. We cannot express our appreciation enough for the way you have translated our vision of space into the graphic language of this book. Judith Nasatir, thank you for helping us find our voice in the written word.

THOMAS HICKEY

Candace, my soul mate, you make it all possible and worthwhile. Thank you for your invaluable support since the beginning, when all we had was a dream and a Le Corbusier table to work from. My daughters Evelyn and Annette, you are my two greatest treasures, and I am eternally smitten. I am so grateful to and thankful for my mother and father, whose love, affection, and encouragement shaped me into the curious architect I am today. Last but not least, there is Eddie. Ours is an adventure that could never have been scripted. We have traveled the world designing amazing projects for incredible people. I am proud and honored to call you my partner.

EDWARD YEDID

Sally, you are a true force. My wife, my life partner, my inspiration, I admire your capacity for love and compassion. I am forever grateful for the way you challenge me to try new things, for they have led to greater successes in all aspects of life and design. My daughter, Marilyn, you have already taught me so much about patience and unconditional love. I will cherish your sweet, innocent heart forever. My parents have my love and deepest appreciation for providing endless opportunities, unconditional support, and joyful exposure to the world and all its beauty. Tom, I have learned so much from you over the years, and I am so grateful to have you as a mentor and friend. It is wonderful to enjoy what this very special life of design has provided us.

PHOTOGRAPHY CREDITS

Photographs by Richard Powers
Except as noted below

William Abranowicz: 74, 75, 79, 83, 92, 93, 97, 219, 220, 221, 222-23, 225, 226, 227, 228, 229, 230, 231, 233, 234-35, 237, 238, 239, 240, 241, 242, 243, 244, 245, 246, 249, 250, 251

Federica Carlet: 252, 253

Francis Dzikowski/Otto: 8-9

First published in the United States by The Monacelli Press

Library of Congress Control Number: 2019940440

ISBN: 978-158093-553-1

Design: Doug Turshen with Steve Turner

Printed in China

The Monacelli Press
6 West 18th Street
New York, New York 10011